HOW-TO SERIES

for the HR Professional

Mastering Market Data

Jane Bjorndal McAdams
Linda K. Ison, CCP

About WorldatWork®

WorldatWork is the world's leading not-for-profit professional association dedicated to knowledge leadership in total rewards, compensation, benefits and work-life. Founded in 1955, WorldatWork focuses on human resources disciplines associated with attracting, motivating and retaining employees. Besides serving as the membership association of the professions, the WorldatWork family of organizations provides education, certification (Certified Compensation Professional – CCP®, Certified Benefits Professional® – CBP, Global Remuneration Professional – GRP® and Work-Life Certified Professional – WLCP™), publications, knowledge resources, surveys, conferences, research and networking. WorldatWork Society of Certified Professionals®, Alliance for Work-Life Progress (AWLP)™ and ITAC, The Telework Advisory Group, are part of the WorldatWork family.

WorldatWork®

The Professional Association for Compensation, Benefits and Total Rewards

WorldatWork
14040 N. Northsight Blvd., Scottsdale, AZ 85260
480/951-9191   Fax 480/483-8352
www.worldatwork.org

Publishing Manager: Dan Cafaro
Graphic Design: Mark Anthony Muñoz
Production Manager: Rebecca Williams Ficker
Staff Contributor: Andrea Ozias

Table of Contents

Introduction

A prime objective for most organizations' compensation management programs is to be "externally competitive." However, the mechanism used to measure competitiveness can differ from company to company, change within the same organization over time or reflect the individual viewpoints of the compensation practitioner performing the analysis.

For example, a major manufacturing employer in a small-business community will view the market from a different perspective than a struggling service company in the same area. Or a company may define its competitive objectives differently in a high-profit-margin environment than when its financial performance is faltering. Finally, one compensation manager might select different survey sources than another as a basis for making competitive pricing decisions.

The goal of "market pricing" is to compile data to meet the organiztional objective of external competitiveness. Market pricing clearly is not an exact science. However, using too much "artistic license" with data analyses may leave the results open to challenge.

In this booklet, guidelines are suggested that add structure and validity to the market-pricing process. Examples of data analyses related to market pricing are provided. The guidelines and examples focus on base pay analyses and are discussed from the perspective of an emerging practitioner. Also included is a discussion of the incorporation of market-pricing results into the administration of a base pay program.

The issues related to designing and conducting a custom compensation survey are addressed in the WorldatWork publication *Measuring the Marketplace: An Approach to Designing and Conducting a Salary Survey.* The material in this booklet assumes that pay data from specific survey sources already have been analyzed statistically — whether from an in-house survey or from surveys conducted by external parties. For our analyses, we have access to **summary statistics** derived from these custom and published surveys. In addition, while survey sources may deal with data such as merit budgets and prevalence of perquisites, this discussion focuses primarily on the analysis of base pay.

1

Defining Compensation Philosophy and Market-Pricing Strategies

Y our organization's compensation philosophy and policies normally will be reflected in your strategies for market pricing, revealed by your answers to the following kinds of questions:

- What are your organization's criteria for identifying the "competition" (industry type, organization size, geographic location)? Which is most important, and does prioritization change by job group?

- What "target" market position will be monitored by your organization relative to your competitors (average, 50th percentile and/or 75th percentile)? Will this be monitored by base salary and/or total compensation? Does the targeted position change by job group?

- How will midpoints of the pay structure(s) be positioned relative to this marketplace (structure policy)?

- What is the targeted comparison of actual employee pay versus this marketplace (pay policy)?

Translating Concepts into Statements

Following are some examples of translating these philosophical concepts into market-pricing policy statements.

- *"As a pharmaceutical manufacturer with annual revenues of approximately $2.5 billion, we define our competitors by the following categories for the job groups identified in Figure 1."*

- *"Relative to our competitor group, we monitor market-rate data as shown in Figure 2."*

- *"Our structure policy for all structures is a lead-lag position relative to the targeted marketplace."* (Structure policies are discussed in detail in WorldatWork Certification Course T3: Quantitative Methods. A "lead-lag" policy positions pay structure midpoints so they match the market midyear. They lead the external market for the first half of the fiscal year and lag the market for the second half.)

- *"Our pay policy is to keep our actual pay levels directly competitive with our targeted marketplace competition for each identified job group."*

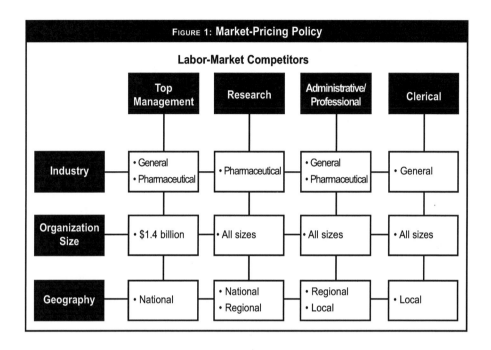

FIGURE 1: **Market-Pricing Policy**

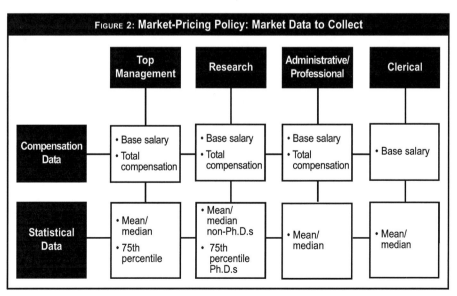

FIGURE 2: **Market-Pricing Policy: Market Data to Collect**

2

Selecting and
Reviewing Survey Sources

H aving defined strategies and policies for the market-pricing program, employers generally select survey sources on the basis of criteria such as:

Fit to Market-Pricing Strategy

- Does the survey provide data in a format that supports your criteria for targeting competitors and collecting market data? (For example, are data reported by industry groups, by geographic area, for 50th and 75th percentiles?)

Quality of Data

- Is the survey sponsor reputable? Are you comfortable with the quality of data verification and analysis procedures?

- Are the survey job descriptions adequate for good job matching?

- How large is the survey sample? Did a sufficient number of your labor-market competitors participate in the survey?

- If this is an annual survey, are the data reliable? (There should not be wide swings in the reported statistics from year to year.)

When all sources have been selected and assembled, you should review each source and record information.

Availability

- Can the survey data you want be obtained by participating in or purchasing a survey?

- Does the timing of the publication of survey results meet your needs?

Cost

- Based on the criteria identified here, does the survey provide enough benefit and value to justify the expense?

- In some instances, the "cost" of the survey simply is the time taken to complete the survey questionnaire; survey reports are provided to participants on a complimentary basis. At the other extreme is the survey available exclusively to a select group of participants who submit data *and* pay a survey fee. An in-between option is the survey that can be purchased regardless of whether data are submitted. In most cases, such surveys feature a reduced fee schedule for participants.

When all sources have been selected and assembled, you should review each source and record information such as the following:

- General points. Note the publisher, phone contact, number of participants and definitions applied in the survey. Some or all of this information will be used when interpreting results.

- Effective date of survey data. This information will be used to compute a trending factor.

- Quality factor. Based on overall quality, a "weighting" factor will be developed and used to value one source in comparison with others when market-rate composites are computed across multiple sources.

3

Matching to Jobs
in Survey Sources

Internal jobs that can be matched to those in the survey sources generally are referred to as "benchmark" jobs. Benchmark jobs are key or critical positions, often multi-incumbent, that span the current pay hierarchy and represent all major job families. Benchmark matches should be based on job content in comparison with the survey job description. Matches generally should not be made based on the position's title only. As a guideline, if you estimate that 70 percent or more of the job content is similar, the match may be considered good.

A job may be matched to more than one set of statistics in the same survey, depending on the information reported.

The selection of market rates from any published source should be guided by pre-established policies. For example, only mean/median base salary data might be extracted for clerical jobs, while mean/median and 75th-percentile base salary and total compensation data might be extracted for top-management jobs.

A job may be matched to more than one set of statistics in the same survey, depending on the information reported. Some surveys display statistics based on multiple "cuts" of the data for the same position — summaries by industry, revenue size and geographic area, for instance. In this case, a clerical job may be matched only in a geographic category, while a management job might be matched in both an industry and a revenue-size category.

If regression equations are included in the survey, the match still should be based on a job-content comparison with the job description. Decisions then need to be made as to which equation(s) to use (if several are included for a job) and the value of the scope data (annual sales volume, for example) for the equation(s). The use of regression equations to obtain market rates is discussed in more detail later in this booklet.

It is not typical that one benchmark job is matched to two different job titles in the same survey. If the position in your organization combines duties described in two separate survey job descriptions, it is difficult to reliably price your position based on the market data for the two survey jobs. You cannot combine the data additively, and you cannot be sure of the true market value for one job assuming the duties of both positions.

Some compensation analysts apply a job-specific "adjustment" factor to increase or decrease the market data based on the perceived degree of match. For example, an analyst might choose to increase the market data by 5 percent to adjust for the fact that the internal job has a higher experience requirement than the survey job. This technique should be used with discretion, as it leaves the analyst open to challenges regarding the objectivity of the final market rates.

Another consideration is the quality of the job match. For example, a job can be matched in three sources but the analyst may feel that the match is significantly better in the first source. In computing the final market-rate composite from these three sources, data from the first source might be given more weight than data extracted from the other two sources.

4

Interpreting Published Data

I nterpretation of published survey data is complicated by the fact that
survey administrators can choose different approaches to collecting,
analyzing and displaying survey results. The challenges at this point in
the market-pricing exercise are to make sound decisions as to which data to
extract from a particular source and to interpret these data appropriately
when they are analyzed across several sources.

To facilitate the discussion, let's examine a case study depicting two
variations in sampling and publishing survey data. Although the example
deals with a minimum amount of data, it points out some of the subtleties
of analyzing and interpreting the market data. (In addition, this is the type
of analysis that might be performed if you conducted an in-house survey.)

Note that the "interquartile range" in the case study is calculated as the
difference between the third quartile (75th percentile) and the first quartile
(25th percentile) of the published data. More detailed definitions of other
statistical terms are included in WorldatWork's *Measuring the Marketplace*.

Case Study of Interpreting Market Data

Five local companies are hiring in the marketplace for the same job. Two
third-party surveys are conducted using different data-collection approaches.
These two parties publish the results as shown in Figures 3 (see page 21)
and 4 (see page 22).

Major Points to Note

What are the major points to note in comparing and interpreting the two sets
of published statistics for this job?

Mean

Survey 1 uses the term "mean" to reflect a simple average across all employees
in the job. The averages per company are neither computed nor reported in
this analysis. Using the published results from Survey 1, you cannot do a
relative comparison of pay practices treating each company equally. If one

FIGURE 3: Survey Scenario 1

Data-collection approach: Actual salaries are collected for all employees in the job from each of the five companies.

Survey Database		Survey Analysis	
Company 1:	$20,000		$16,000
	22,000		18,500
	22,500		19,000
	23,500	25th Percentile ❷	20,000
			22,000
Company 2:	23,000		22,000
	31,000		22,000
		50th Percentile ❷	22,500
Company 3:	16,000		22,500
			23,000
Company 4:	18,500		23,000
	19,000	75th Percentile ❷	23,500
	22,500		24,000
			29,000
Company 5:	22,000		31,000
	22,000		
	23,000	Mean =	$22,533
	24,000		
	29,000	Cases (n) =	15

Published Results

25th Percentile	Median	Median	75th Percentile	Number of Cases
$20,000	$22,500	$22,533	$23,500	15

Interquartile range: $23,500 − $20,000 = $3,500

company had a large number of employees in the sample, its data could overly influence the statistics and the analyst could not discern this fact when reviewing only the published results.

Figure 4: Survey Scenario 2

Survey Database		
	Avg.	No. of Employees
Company 1:	$22,000	4
Company 2:	27,000	2
Company 3:	16,000	1
Company 4:	20,000	3
Company 5:	24,000	5

Survey Analysis						
				n		Weighted Amount
		$16,000	x	1	=	$16,000
25th Percentile						
		20,000	x	3	=	60,000
50th Percentile		22,000	x	4	=	88,000
		24,000	x	5	=	120,000
75th Percentile						
		27,000	x	2	=	54,000
		Company				Weighted
Means	=	$21,800				$22,533
Cases (n) =		5				15

Published Results

25th Percentile	Median	Weighted Mean	Median	75th Percentile	Number of Employees	Number of Companies
$18,000	$22,000	$22,533	$21,800	$25,500	15	5

Interquartile range: $25,500 – $18,000 = $7,500

In comparing the surveys, the Survey 1 "mean" actually is the same statistic as reported under the heading "weighted mean" in Survey 2 — the average pay for all incumbents in the job. The data shown under the "mean" column of Survey 2 actually is the company mean — information that was not provided in Survey 1. In neither situation is the terminology misused. A difference exists in analytic techniques, and the analyst must be aware of this difference when using data from these two sources.

Percentiles

The difference between the percentiles reported in the two sources might best be captured by translating the data for one percentile (the 25th, for example) into statements such as the following:

- Based on the Survey 1 sample: "25 percent of the employees in the job make less than $20,000."

- Based on the Survey 2 sample: "In 25 percent of the companies, the average pay for the job is less than $18,000."

Using the published results from Survey 2, you can make no inferences about the distribution of the actual pay of the employees in the job. These percentiles describe only company averages.

In the two survey scenarios, the difference between the interquartile ranges ($3,500 in Scenario 1 versus $7,500 in Scenario 2) is a result of the data-collection and analysis techniques, not of an actual differential in market pay for the job. If you were trying to reconcile the difference or select one value to use, understanding the nuances of the data analyses could be the key to making a sound market-pricing decision.

General Guidelines

How does this translate into general guidelines? It is clear that survey statistics are affected by the way the data are collected. The key is to be sure you understand the way the statistics are computed in any given survey. If this is not specifically documented in the survey report, contact the survey publisher to verify computations.

It is important to note the following when interpreting survey data:

- Measures of central tendency (mean and median) typically are less affected by the kinds of sampling variations depicted in the prior examples. However, as samples get smaller, even these statistics can be adversely affected.

- A large difference between mean and median statistics can be the result of a sample that is skewed high or low by a few unusual cases. Means are affected by such skewing; medians are not. Which statistic to use is still a matter of choice. However, unless you have a high degree of confidence in the sampling and the data analyses, you may choose the median as the better estimate of the "typical" pay for the job.

- Use of a mean versus a weighted mean when both are given also is a matter of choice. However, the choice should be backed by a defined strategy either of giving equal weight to every employee represented in the survey sample (the weighted mean) or of giving equal weight to each company represented in the sample (the unweighted or company mean).

The decision to use one or the other statistic need not be applied globally to all survey sources. For example, if you are using a local survey source for nonexempt jobs, and you are familiar with and in direct competition with all companies included in the survey sample, you may choose to use the weighted mean as the statistic most representative of the market rate for the job. (You recruit from basically the same applicant pool as other companies in the sample.)

If your survey source is a broad national survey that presents data in geographic categories, you may choose to use the company or unweighted mean as the representative market rate. In this case, you cannot be sure what companies or employee data are represented in the sample.

The decision to use one or the other statistic need not be applied globally to all survey sources.

Generally, you would not mix the statistics selected from one source. In the preceding example, you would extract weighted means for all jobs in the first source and company means for all jobs in the second source.

- It is important to consider the range (or dispersion) of the data. The standard deviation is a statistic that is useful in analyzing data dispersion. However, the standard deviation is not commonly included in published survey summaries. From a more practical standpoint, you often can calculate the range (highest reported value minus lowest reported value) or, as shown in the previous case study, you can calculate the interquartile range.

- If regression equations are included in a survey report, you have to evaluate the equations for your matched jobs at the appropriate scope value to obtain estimated market-rate data. Figure 5 provides a typical illustration of this procedure.

In using and interpreting regression estimates, the following guidelines are helpful:

– Be certain the scope data you are using to evaluate the regression model are within the range of the scope data appropriate to the model. This range usually is depicted graphically (the beginning and ending points of the regression line) in survey reports.

– Evaluating an equation at more than one value will give you a better understanding of the variance in the survey sample. In Figure 5, it may be helpful to evaluate the equation at $1 billion and $5 billion, in addition to your job's scope of $2.5 billion, to derive comparison points for your estimated salary.

– You should refer to regression statistics such as the r-square (coefficient of determination) and the standard error of estimate (SEE) to determine how "good" a regression estimate is. Refer to an introductory statistical text (or materials for WorldatWork Certification Course T3) for details on these statistics and their interpretation.

FIGURE 5: **Example of Using a Survey-Regression Equation**

Job
Chief Financial Officer

Scope of Job
Company Revenue = $2.5 Billion

Survey-Regression Model Matched for Chief Financial Officer
Log (Base Salary) = 4.828 + 0.1694 x Log (revenue in millions)

Evaluating the Model for Your Scope Revenue

Log (Base Salary)	= 4.828 + 0.1694 x Log (2,500)
	= 4.828 + 0.1694 x 3.3979
	= 4.828 + 0.5756
	= 5.4036
Base Salary	= Log – 1 (5.4036)
	= $253,286

Notes

1) The "Log – 1" function inverts the log value. It is equivalent to the value of 105.4036. These computations can be performed on many pocket calculators.

2) The salary of $253,286 is the estimated mean annual base salary for a chief financial officer in a company with revenue of $2.5 billion.

–   Note that a regression equation built on actual salary data for job incumbents estimates mean salaries. A regression model cannot generate true 25th and 75th percentiles of actual salaries for the sample. (Certain statistical statements can be made based on the standard error of the estimate and assumptions about the sample distribution. However, these "percentile" statements must be interpreted differently than true percentiles based on the actual survey sample.)

In summary, regarding the interpretation of published survey data, without source data (which rarely are published in survey reports), it often is difficult to reconstruct what is causing variations in market rates between different sources. The more you know about the survey, the more reliable the decisions you can make using the data.

5

Determining Market-Rate Composites

The final step in compiling market-rate data for a job is developing a "market rate composite"— the most representative market figure or value for a benchmark job. This value also is known as the "going rate" or "market consensus" for the job.

The market-rate composite will reflect market-pricing decisions already made in selecting appropriate surveys and survey statistics and in matching your jobs to survey jobs. Two additional issues should be considered in computing market-rate composites:

- "Trending" (updating or "aging") the survey data to one point in time

- Weighting market-rate data across survey sources.

Trending Survey Data

It is important to trend published survey data to one common point in time so that accurate and consistent market comparisons can be made between the market and internal average pay.

Important considerations in selecting an annual trending factor and the date to which you want to trend include the following:

- Compensation levels increase at different rates in the marketplace. For example, the rate of increase in executive pay generally exceeds the rate of increase in nonexempt pay on an average annual basis. Consequently, you should research market movement based on considerations such as the following:

  - Industry type: health care, finance, manufacturing, service, etc.

  - Job level: nonexempt, exempt or executive

  - Geographic location: Northeast, Midwest, South, etc.

  - Type of compensation: base salary or total compensation.

- To select an appropriate annual trending factor (for example, increase nonexempt data by 4 percent and executive data by 5 percent), you can review surveys that present data on annual-increase budgets such as the

WorldatWork *Salary Budget Survey*. This approach assumes that actual pay in the labor market increases by the budgeted increase amount. There are some challenges to this assumption — "slippage" or "wash-out" — which are discussed in other WorldatWork publications and courses. (See Figure 6.)

- Another source of market movement is the year-over-year increase in mean/median market rates within a single survey source. Such data often

Figure 6: Sample Calculation of Trending Market Rates

To trend a market rate of $24,075 from September 1999 (survey date) to July 2000 (lead-lag policy for fiscal year beginning in January), assuming a 4-percent annual increase factor in 1999 and a 5-percent factor in 2000, complete these steps:

- Calculate the 1999 trending percentage (4 months):
  $\frac{4}{12} \times 4\% = 1.33\%$ (or a factor of 1.0133)

- Calculate the 2000 trending percentage (6 months):
  $\frac{6}{12} \times 5\% = 2.5\%$ (or a factor of 1.025)

- Using these percentages as multiplicative factors, compound the factors across the two years to develop the total trending factor or percentage:
  $1.0133 \times 1.025 = 1.03863$ (or 3.86% as a total trending percentage)

- Multiply the market rate by the trending factor:
  $24,075 \times 1.03863 = 25,006$

- Consequently, the $23,879 market rate as of September 1999 becomes $25,006 when projected to July 2000.

are reported in the introduction or executive summary of surveys. This change in mean/median market rates is one of the most accurate measures of market movement. However, the increases are historical rather than projected. (Cautions associated with this approach include ensuring that changes in the survey participant group do not unduly in-fluence changes in market rates.)

- To trend data across two calendar years, you should develop a separate trending figure for each year and then combine (compound) the two percentages.

- The lead, lead-lag or lag structure policy will determine to what point in time you should trend your survey data for purposes of establishing competitive pay structure midpoints. For example, if your fiscal year is January through December and your policy is lead-lag, you will trend all data to July 1.

- In using market data to compare with current incumbent pay levels, you may want to trend market data to the current date. This allows you to compare actual pay in your organization "today" with competitive market pay representative of "today." (If projections into the future are to be made, you also may trend both the survey data and incumbent pay data to the same future date.)

Weighting Market-Rate Data Across Survey Sources

A decision regarding weighting survey data will be a function of a number of criteria, including the following:

- **Compensation strategy**. For example, you will weight surveys in your industry more heavily if you have established a strategy that defines your competitive labor market as industry-specific.

- **Quality of surveys.** The statistical analyses provided — participant base and number of cases per job, among other factors — contribute to the perceived quality of a survey. Based on judgments about this quality, some surveys will receive more weight than others. For example, if one of your sources is a survey you conducted in-house, you may choose to weight this source more heavily than sources obtained externally.

- **Quality of job match.** Certain job matches are more appropriate than others based on job content, and market data can be weighted accordingly. This job-specific weighting factor can supplement or override previously established survey-source weights. To generate an objective weighting factor at the job level, the number of cases (employees or companies) can be used to weight the raw data.

Based on judgments about quality, some surveys will receive more weight than others.

Surveys that most accurately capture your labor market and best reflect your jobs' contents — and provide accurate and appropriate statistical analyses — are those to which you will give the most weight.

In Figure 7 on page 31, each survey is assigned a weighting factor (in this case, a proportion of 100 percent). The survey market rates then are multiplied by this weight, and the sum of the products yields the market-rate composite.

FIGURE 7: Sample Calculation of Weighting Market Rates			
Survey	Market Rate	Survey Weight	Market Rate Weighted Product
1	$25,006	20%	$25,006 × .20 = $5,001
2	23,748	40	23,748 × .40 = 9,499
3	20,500	40	20,500 × .40 = 8,200
Market-Rate Composite: $5,001 + $9,499 + $8,200 = $22,700			

Combining the two concepts of trending and weighting survey data, we now can develop common-date market-rate composites per job as shown in Figure 8 on page 32. The assumptions for the calculations are as follows:

- The company's salary-structure policy is lead-lag, and the fiscal year is January to December.

- The trending percentage for exempt jobs is 4 percent for 1999 and 5 percent for 2000; for executive jobs (including controller), the percentage is 4.5 percent for 1999 and 5.5 percent for 2000.

It is helpful to keep in mind some general observations regarding the types of computations depicted here:

- In developing market-rate composites, it is preferable to have three or four survey sources.

- The use of different trending figures for different years becomes more important as the estimated market movement becomes more dramatic — for instance, a shift from 4 percent to 7 percent.

- In this example, Survey 2 is weighted at 40 percent in all composites, indicating that it is judged to be of high quality for all matches. Typically, there is a fair amount of similarity in the weighting of one survey compared to others — the quality of the statistical analyses and the participant base, for instance, are constant for the survey regardless of the job matched. The survey would, therefore, carry the same general weight for most matched jobs.

Our example is restricted to developing one market-rate composite (average base pay) for each job. However, based on your organization's compensation philosophy and market-pricing strategy, you may compute more than one such composite. For example, if your strategy is to track the market at total compensation as well as base salary, or at 75th percentile as

FIGURE 8: Sample of Developing Market-Rates Composites

Job Title: Personnel Representative

Survey	Effective Date of Survey Data	Survey & Match Quality	Original Market Rate
1	Sept. 1999	M	$33,705
2	Jan. 2000	H	32,465
3	Aug. 1999	H	27,544

Job Title: Controller

Survey	Effective Date of Survey Data	Survey & Match Quality	Original Market Rate
2	Jan. 2000	H	$59,633
4	Feb. 2000	M	62,922
5	Oct. 1999	M	61,355

Job Title: Registered Nurse

Survey	Effective Date of Survey Data	Survey & Match Quality	Original Market Rate
2	Jan. 2000	H	$35,599
6	Dec. 1999	L	44,481
7	July 1999	M	37,129
8	Aug. 1999	M	34,258

well as mean/median, you would collect survey data and calculate market-rate composites for each independently.

Developing the market-rate composite by trending and then weighting survey data can be as simple or as complicated as you desire. For those who have access to microcomputers, this is an application that easily can be supported by spreadsheet software.

Total Trending Percent	Trended Market Rate	Survey Weight	Weighted Product
3.86%	$35,006	20%	$ 7,001
2.50%	33,277	40%	13,311
4.21%	28,703	40%	11,481

Market-Rate Composite (as of July 2000) = $31,793

Total Trending Percent	Trended Market Rate	Survey Weight	Weighted Product
2.75%	$61,273	40%	$24,509
2.29%	64,363	30%	19,309
3.90%	63,748	30%	19,124

Market-Rate Composite (as of July 2000) = $62,942

Total Trending Percent	Trended Market Rate	Survey Weight	Weighted Product
2.50%	$36,489	40%	$14,596
2.84%	45,744	10%	4,574
4.55%	38,819	25%	9,705
4.21%	35,700	25%	8,925

Market-Rate Composite (as of July 2000) = $37,800

6

Making Policy
and Program Decisions

Market-rate composites provide an accurate reading of pay competitiveness in the labor markets (and, consequently, establish targets for internal compensation programs). We now can use this information to analyze our current situation and make appropriate changes. This section discusses how survey data and market-rate composites are used in the following ways:

- **Determining the competitiveness of current pay using:**
    - The market index
    - Regression analysis.

- **Developing a competitive pay line and corresponding pay structure using:**
    - Market consensus by grade as midpoints
    - The "present value/future value" concept to develop midpoints
    - Regression analysis to develop midpoints.

- **Adjusting or updating a current pay structure.**

Determining the Competitiveness of Current Pay

Market Index. Determining the competitiveness of current pay is an extremely important application of survey results. The examples in Figures 9 (see page 38) and 10 (see page 39) display one way comparisons to market can be made.

Note the following:

- In these figures, the ratio of internal pay to market is calculated by dividing the actual salary by the market rate. This is called a "market index." ("Market index" should not be confused with "compa-ratio," which is the ratio of actual pay to structure midpoint.)

- Data are grouped by job family, so comparisons on market competitiveness can be made across job families. A job-family market index is "weighted" by the number of internal employees per job (that is, "weighted-average actual salary" divided by "weighted market-rate composite"). In this example, the nursing department, with an index of 110 percent, is positioned the highest relative to the market. Management Information Systems, with an index of 90 percent, has the lowest market position.

- Data also are summarized by management and nonmanagement market indices, with the nonmanagement group being paid slightly more competitively.

- Only base pay comparisons are made. Similar comparisons for total compensation can be made when such data are collected.

How should an organization interpret the results of this analysis? How do you know if jobs and incumbents are paid competitively? Answering these questions appropriately requires thoughtful review and interpretation of the data in relation to issues such as the following:

- **Design of the current salary structure.** For instance, in an executive structure with 60-percent range spreads, a market index of 81 percent for a single incumbent job may be acceptable. The same market index could indicate a potential problem for a multi-incumbent job in a nonexempt structure with 40-percent range spreads.

- **Nature of the job.** Some jobs serve as entry-level positions through which employees pass quickly. Thus, job tenure is low and turnover is high. If employees typically are hired at grade minimum or low in the range, the job will have a low market index — a situation that is both expected and acceptable, assuming you can attract adequate numbers of qualified candidates.

- **Type of job evaluation plan.** If the company uses a "market pricing and slotting" evaluation plan, a job with a high or low market index can simply be reslotted into a different grade based on market-pricing results. If, however, the company uses a factor-based evaluation system, a job with a very high or low market index may have to be "red-circled" or "green-circled" to ensure the continued internal equity of all jobs.

- **Number of incumbents in the job.** It is more typical for a heavily populated job to have a normal distribution of pay and, therefore, to be paid closer to the market-rate composite. Consequently, in a bank, a market index of 83 percent for the teller job will be of greater concern than the same index for the single-incumbent accounting manager job.

Figure 9: Using the Market Index to Determine Competitiveness of Current Pay

Grade	Number of Job Title	Average Actual Employees	Market-Rate Salary	Market Composite	Index
1	Personnel Representative	4	$27,440	$31,793	86%
3	Sr. Compensation Analyst	2	35,980	39,200	92%
4	Security Supervisor*	1	46,200	46,900	99%
5	Manager, Training*	1	57,400	55,300	104%
6	Director, Human Resources*	1	63,000	61,600	102%
	Overall Market Index (Human Resources): 94%				
1	Accounting Assistant	10	$28,000	$29,400	95%
2	Accountant	6	33,600	34,300	98%
3	Accounting Supervisor*	3	44,100	42,000	105%
5	Internal Auditor	1	53,200	53,200	100%
6	Controller*	1	67,200	62,942	107%
	Overall Market Index (Finance): 99%				
1	LPN	25	$30,800	$28,000	110%
2	Registered Nurse	100	41,300	37,800	109%
3	Nursing Instructor	10	48,300	42,700	113%
3	Nurse Supervisor*	5	53,200	49,000	109%
6	Director, Emergency Room*	1	66,500	53,900	123%
	Overall Market Index (Nursing): 110%				
1	Programmer	6	$29,400	$37,100	79%
2	Data Entry Supervisor*	4	32,900	35,700	92%
4	Systems Analyst	2	42,000	44,800	94%
5	Mgr., Computer Operations*	1	53,200	51,100	104%
6	Director, MIS*	1	66,500	64,400	103%
	Overall Market Index (MIS): 90%				

* Overall Market Index for Management: 104%
Overall Market Index for Nonmanagement: 108%

- **Individual incumbent characteristics.** Employee factors such as education, skill, ability, seniority and individual performance also must be considered when interpreting the comparison of market-rate composites with internal pay levels. It is acceptable and desirable to pay incumbents above or below market composites on the basis of such individual characteristics.

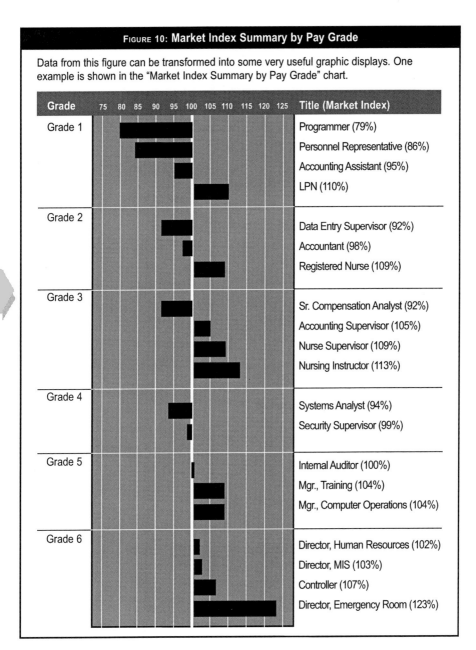

Figure 10: Market Index Summary by Pay Grade

Data from this figure can be transformed into some very useful graphic displays. One example is shown in the "Market Index Summary by Pay Grade" chart.

Grade	75	80	85	90	95	100	105	110	115	120	125	Title (Market Index)
Grade 1												Programmer (79%)
												Personnel Representative (86%)
												Accounting Assistant (95%)
												LPN (110%)
Grade 2												Data Entry Supervisor (92%)
												Accountant (98%)
												Registered Nurse (109%)
Grade 3												Sr. Compensation Analyst (92%)
												Accounting Supervisor (105%)
												Nurse Supervisor (109%)
												Nursing Instructor (113%)
Grade 4												Systems Analyst (94%)
												Security Supervisor (99%)
Grade 5												Internal Auditor (100%)
												Mgr., Training (104%)
												Mgr., Computer Operations (104%)
Grade 6												Director, Human Resources (102%)
												Director, MIS (103%)
												Controller (107%)
												Director, Emergency Room (123%)

- **Accuracy of survey data.** Factors such as sample size, participant base, statistical analyses, survey methodology and job-matching procedures impact the accuracy of the final market-rate composite for a benchmark job. Although we work very hard at it, in fact, there is no exact or perfect market value for a job. As a rule of thumb, when done well, salary survey information is expected to be accurate within plus or minus 5 percent. Consequently, a market index of 95 percent to 105 percent can be viewed as fully meeting competitive market-pay levels.

Based on considerations of this nature, you must decide if the variance from market is explainable and acceptable. In some cases, the variance cannot be explained by reviewing these issues. This might suggest a need to return to the market-rate analysis to verify survey sources and job matches. If, after verification of market data, we still find a large variance between actual and market, decisions for action need to be made to bring actual pay more in line with the market.

For instance, from our previous example, consider the director of emergency room with a market index of 123 percent. Assume that the salary-range spread for the director's grade is 60 percent and that this incumbent has had consistently superior performance with 10 years of seniority in the job. Based on this information, the market index of 123 percent is acceptable and no action needs to be taken.

Regression Analysis. A second technique for obtaining a good picture of overall pay competitiveness for benchmark jobs is to develop a regression of current pay (Y-axis) with market-rate composites (X-axis).

If current pay were to equal the market exactly, the regression line would have a correlation of 1.00. In this case, the plot of the "line of best fit" would lie on the graph at an exact 45-degree angle — that is, a line with a slope of 1.0 and a Y-intercept of 0.0.

In Figure 11 on page 41, one line represents the 100-percent correlation of pay to market, and another line depicts the regression line for current internal pay levels.

Sample size is important in developing this type of analysis. As explained in WorldatWork's *Measuring the Marketplace*, at least 10 data points are needed to perform regression analysis. In our example, we use all 20 benchmark jobs to develop a single comparative regression line. Trying to generate this type of regression line at the departmental level would be inappropriate because of the small number of cases in our example. Basing such an analysis on too small a sample has the potential of producing unreliable results.

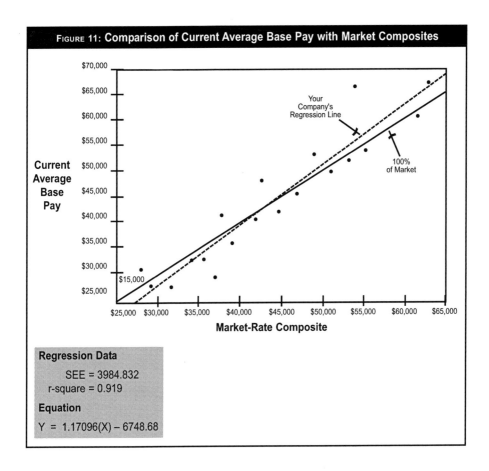

FIGURE 11: Comparison of Current Average Base Pay with Market Composites

Current Average Base Pay

$70,000
$65,000
$60,000
$55,000
$50,000
$45,000
$40,000
$35,000
$30,000
$25,000

$15,000

Your Company's Regression Line

100% of Market

$25,000 $30,000 $35,000 $40,000 $45,000 $50,000 $55,000 $60,000 $65,000

Market-Rate Composite

Regression Data
SEE = 3984.832
r-square = 0.919

Equation
$Y = 1.17096(X) - 6748.68$

Developing a Competitive Pay Line and Corresponding Pay Structure

Three approaches to developing a pay structure are discussed here:

- Using grade-market consensus as the actual grade midpoints
- Using the "present value/future value" concept to develop midpoints
- Using regression analysis to develop midpoints.

Figure 12 (see page 42) shows the data to be used in all three examples of pay-structure development. These examples assume that the grade-assignment decision for each job has been based on an internal job-evaluation plan (i.e., jobs cannot be regraded based solely on market values).

Grade	Title	Market-Rate Composite	Grade-Market Consensus
1	Personnel Representative	$31,793	$31,573
1	Accounting Assistant	29,400	
1	LPN	28,000	
1	Programmer	37,100	
2	Accountant	34,300	35,933
2	Registered Nurse	37,800	
2	Data Entry Supervisor	35,700	
3	Sr. Compensation Analyst	39,200	43,225
3	Accounting Supervisor	42,000	
3	Nursing Instructor	42,700	
3	Nurse Supervisor	49,000	
4	Security Supervisor	46,900	45,850
4	Systems Analyst	44,800	
5	Manager Training	55,300	53,200
5	Internal Auditor	53,200	
5	Manager Computer Operations	51,100	
6	Director, Human Resources	61,600	60,711
6	Controller	62,942	
6	Director, Emergency Room	53,900	
6	Director, MIS	64,400	

FIGURE 12: **Preparing to Use Market Data to Develop a Structure**

Using Market Consensus by Grade as Midpoints

In the first example, the simple average or consensus of the market-rate composites by grade is used as the exact midpoint for the pay structure. Using the sample data, this approach results in the midpoints shown in Figure 13 (see page 43).

This design methodology may result in a structure with administrative and internal equity problems. For instance, because of the 20-percent midpoint differential, a promotion from grade 2 to 3 may be difficult and costly. (If we assumed a 40-percent range spread, an employee would have to be paid above the midpoint of grade 2 to reach the minimum of grade 3.) Likewise, the 6-percent differential between grades 3 and 4 could result in compression problems.

Using the "Present Value/Future Value" Concept to Develop Midpoints

Designing a pay structure with grade-to-grade midpoint increments that follow a geometric progression can reduce some of the administrative problems identified in the previous example.

This simple but effective method applies the "present value/future value" concept to generate a structure with constant percentage increments between all grade midpoints. The application of this method to the sample data is displayed in the example in Figure 14.

Present Value (PV)/Future Value (FV) Formula

$FV = PV \times (1 + i)n$ where:

- FV = the "future value" or midpoint for grade 6 (the highest grade): in this case, $60,711.

- PV = the "present value" or midpoint for grade 1 (the lowest grade): in this case, $31,573.

- i = the "percentage increase rate" or the unknown midpoint-to-midpoint increment to be determined.

FIGURE 13: Example of Using Market Consensus by Grade as Midpoints

Grade	Actual Consensus Midpoint	Midpoint Differential
1	$31,573	
		13.81%
2	35,933	
		20.29%
3	43,225	
		6.07%
4	45,850	
		16.03%
5	53,200	
		14.12%
6	60,711	

FIGURE 14: Example of Using Present Value/Future Value Midpoints

Grade	Actual Consensus Midpoint	Actual Percent Difference	PV/FV Midpoint	Midpoint Differential
1	$31,573		$31,573	
		13.81%		13.97%
2	35,933		35,984	
		20.29%		13.97%
3	43,225		41,011	
		6.07%		13.97%
4	45,850		46,740	
		16.03%		13.97%
5	53,200		53,270	
		14.12%		13.97%
6	60,711		60,711	

- n = the "number of increase intervals": in this case, one less than the total number of grades in the structure, or 5.

Using the sample data, the entire formula and its solution become as follows:

$$\$60,711 = \$31,573 \times (1 + i)^5$$

$$\$60,711 \div \$31,573 = (1 + i)^5$$

$$1.923 = (1 + i)^5$$

$$(1.923)^{1/5} = 1 + i$$

$$1.1397 = 1 + i$$

$$.1397 = i$$

Solving the equation for the unknown value "i" (the midpoint increment) is best accomplished by using a calculator or software to perform mathematical computations. (Many financial calculators have the PV/FV formula preprogrammed.)

The application of the increment value of .1397 (or 13.97 percent) produces the pay-structure midpoints displayed in Figure 14. The midpoints were generated by starting with the first midpoint value of $31,573 and multiplying each midpoint by 1.1397 to derive the midpoint of the next higher grade. (Small variations in computations will be caused by decimal-point rounding.) Because the PV/FV concept has been applied, we can be sure that a $60,711 midpoint will be reached by grade 6.

A third approach to designing midpoints of a pay structure utilizes linear regression analysis.

Using Regression Analysis to Develop Midpoints

A third approach to designing midpoints of a pay structure utilizes linear regression analysis. (See Figure 15 on page 45.) This analysis correlates job market-rate composites (the Y-axis) with pay grades (the X-axis). (Although the point score value per job can be used in this type of analysis, for these next two figures the grade number will be used as the indicator of internal job worth.) Again, the example in Figure 15 uses sample data for the 20 jobs shown previously.

The regression analysis approach develops a pay line (regression "line of best fit") of market rates. Because market data are collected in accordance with your company's compensation philosophy, this regression line can be referred to as your "pay policy line." Using this approach, pay structure midpoints will fall on the pay-policy line.

In the example in Figure 15, the regression slope, Y-intercept and related statistics were derived using software that computes these values based on the data set of 20 cases. Midpoints for each grade are obtained by substituting each grade number (for example, 1 through 6) into the regression equation and solving for the estimated market-rate composite — our proposed grade midpoint. (The calculations for solving the equation are similar to those depicted in the "Example of Using a Survey-Regression Equation" on page 25.) The midpoint differentials were determined after the midpoints were computed and are displayed for reference purposes only.

Following are some observations about the regression analysis approach:

- Because increases in most compensation data are measured in incremental percentages rather than in flat-dollar amounts, we used the Log of the market-rate composites as the Y-variable. Since the Log scale is measured in constant ratios versus constant differences, it is used widely in regressions

---

FIGURE 15: Example of Using Regression Analysis to Develop Midpoints

Model: Market-Rate Composite vs. Pay Grade for All Benchmark Jobs

Regression Equation:

Log (Market-Rate Composite) = 4.44782 + (0.05591 × Pay Grade)

Regression Statistics:

r-square = 0.99

S.E.E. = 0.034

Grade	Actual Consensus Midpoint	Actual Percent Difference	PV/FV Midpoint	Midpoint Differential
1	$31,573		$31,895	
		13.81%		13.74%
2	35,933		36,277	
		20.29%		13.74%
3	43,225		41,262	
		6.07%		13.74%
4	45,850		46,930	
		16.03%		13.74%
5	53,200		53,378	
		14.12%		13.74%
6	60,711		60,712	

involving compensation or financial-scope data. The use of this Log function produces a pay line with a constant increment (geometric progression) between midpoints as shown in our example.

- Our initial set of data was fairly consistent: Few data points were anomalies or "outliers" in comparison with other data points. (For example, a job with a market index of 60 percent would be considered an outlier.) In a "real world" situation, there would be a larger number of jobs and grades — and potentially more outliers. However, in any model, you would expect a small number of cases to fall in this outlier category.

If outliers are identified, you should first verify your data, including the job matches in the survey sources. If the data have been verified and outliers still exist, it then may be appropriate to consider eliminating these outliers and performing the regression analysis again. A single outlier, if extreme enough, can dramatically alter the equation for the line of best fit.

By regenerating the pay line with outliers removed, you can improve your structure design procedure and results in that the following will occur:

- You have more clearly identified problems that perhaps cannot be resolved within the context of your pay structure. Once identified, these unusual benchmark jobs may need to be handled by a special pay policy.

- Your goal is to develop a structure that is competitive for the *majority* of your benchmark jobs and employees. By eliminating outliers, you can model the impact of alternative pay lines to develop a pay structure and midpoints that best achieve your competitive goals.

The Regression Structure display shows the pay policy line and new structure for the regression approach. (See Figure 16 on page 47.) For comparison purposes, the market consensus and average base pay per grade also are included.

In the regression and present value/future value approaches, structures with constant grade-to-grade midpoint differentials were generated. More sophisticated and creative approaches (nonlinear regression analysis, for example) can be applied to generate variable midpoint differentials. These incrementally increasing midpoints achieve two goals: First, they generally better reflect actual changes in market data. Second, they reflect salary structure design principles that suggest it is appropriate to have smaller

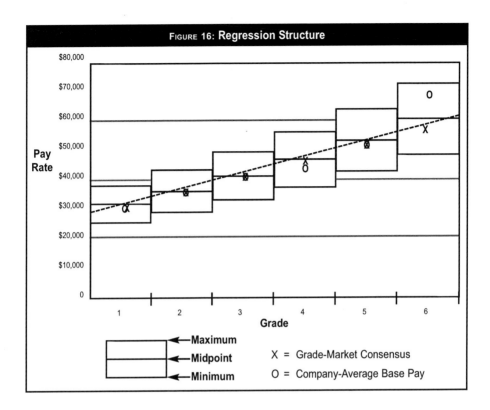

FIGURE 16: Regression Structure

midpoint differentials (perhaps 5 percent to 8 percent) for the lower grades and larger midpoint differentials (perhaps 10 percent to 15 percent) for the higher grades.

All three approaches discussed here are valid ways of developing salary structures, as are several other options. The approach you choose may be in part a function of your degree of comfort with statistical analysis. There are software packages specifically designed for, or easily adapted to, the development of competitive pay structures. These packages can greatly facilitate the analysis and interpretation of the statistical results.

Adjusting or Updating a Current Pay Structure

Thus far, this publication has addressed market-pricing techniques and structure-design approaches in the context of creating a **new pay structure**. These techniques and approaches are equally appropriate for use in updating or maintaining the competitiveness over time of established pay structures.

Each year, new market-rate data are
compiled for benchmark jobs, and a
new structure is developed, independent
of the current year's structure.

To maintain market competitiveness, most organizations revise their pay structures annually or every other year. As with pay-structure design, the goal is to keep structure midpoints on track with market data and to maintain a pay-policy line that supports the organization's competitive pay strategies.

The best way to accomplish this is to use the same principles discussed in relation to building pay structures. Each year, new market-rate data are compiled for benchmark jobs, and a new structure is developed, independent of the current year's structure. From an administrative point of view, this approach is time-consuming. However, the result is a structure that more effectively supports your organization's compensation philosophy and pay policy.

A different approach to adjusting structures — and one with clear limitations — is to research published surveys for data on projected structure-adjustment percentages. For example, if surveys project a 3-percent adjustment for nonexempt structures within your industry, that factor is used to update all range rates in the current structure; each grade of the structure is increased, or "bumped," by 3 percent. This approach captures average movement in structures among the companies participating in the survey — not movement in market rates for individual benchmark jobs. Therefore, over time, this approach does not necessarily keep structure midpoints on track with real market movement.

To address the time-consuming aspect of the first approach, some organizations use a variation that involves performing the detailed analysis every second or third year and adjusting the structure by a percentage bump during the interim year(s). This option works well during years of low inflation, when year-to-year increases in market data are modest and consistent across job groups.

Sound and Practical Guidelines

This booklet has provided sound and practical guidelines for analyzing and using market data to complete basic tasks in establishing and maintaining a competitive base pay program.

However, for every issue highlighted here, dozens of others could be addressed. Understanding and utilizing the basic concepts addressed in this booklet provide a more solid foundation for extending the analyses to more complex external equity issues such as the following:

- Gathering and analyzing pay data and practices at the total cash compensation level (for example, establishing bonus targets or building total compensation pay lines)

- Integrating market data with a job-evaluation plan to design pay structures that blend the concepts of external competitiveness and internal equity

- Performing more advanced statistical analyses to develop pay structures with increasing, rather than constant, midpoint differentials

- Performing detailed cost analyses in relation to issues such as the implementation of new pay structures or the development of merit-increase matrices and salary-increase budgets.

Topics of this nature are discussed to some extent in WorldatWork certification courses and publications.

Whatever methodologies and approaches you use to analyze salary survey data, ensuring that the market-pricing process supports your organization's compensation philosophy and business strategies, as well as making sure that your decisions are made based on a full understanding of the information, will put you well on your way to mastering market data.